The Easter Ballad

Martin Burke

Wordsonthestreet

First published in 2007 by
Wordsonthestreet
Six San Antonio Park,
Salthill,
Galway, Ireland.
web: www.wordsonthestreet.com
email: publisher@wordsonthestreet.com

© Martin Burke

British Library Cataloguing in Publication Data:
A catalogue record for this book is available from the British Library.

ISBN 0-9552604-2-6
978-0-9552604-2-1

All rights reserved. No part of this publication may be reproduced or transmitted in any form or by any means, electronic or mechanical, including photography, recording, or any information storage or retrieval system, without permission in writing from the publisher. The book is sold subject to the condition that it shall not, by way of trade or otherwise, be lent, resold or otherwise circulated without the publisher's prior consent in any form of binding or cover other than that in which it is published and without a similar condition, including this condition, being imposed on the subsequent purchaser.

Cover illustration and design: Wordsonthestreet
Layout and typesetting: Wordsonthestreet
Printed by Lightningsource UK

For Liz and Griet Goddaer

Also by Martin Burke

Poetry
The Other Life FootHills Publishing, NY (2004)
The Weave That Binds Us Inner Circle Publishing, Iowa (2004)
Into History Arabesques Editions, Algeria/USA(2006)
Psalms Default press, Ireland(2006)
Kings (five poems for the theatre) World Audience Publishers, NY(2007)
I Ching Cervena Barva Press, N.Y.

E-books
Triptych Scare Publications
Go Slow Trains Publications
Gilgamesh Cervena Barva Press (Poetry Kit recommendation)
The Navigations of October Independentbook.com
Antigone's Cry (essay) Independentbook.com
The Aran Mass Default Press
Love's Begotten Flame Dreamers of the Day

Plays
Six Scenes From A War New Theatre Publications, UK(2005)
Short plays produced in USA and UK
His version of The Oresteia had a play reading in Brussels
Plays published in Scene4 (USA), Oregon Literary Review (USA), The Roundtable Review(UK) and Electica (UK)

Forthcoming
The Proclamation at Baghdad (Antigone) India, 2007
Everyman Ireland, 2007

Acknowledgements are due to the editors of

> Poetry Salzburg Review
> Scriberazone
> Projected Letters
> Nimble spirit Review
> Delcanto
> WOW!
> Stride
> Contraflower

where most of these poems first appeared

Poetry?
that was the voice which did not interfere
with how each thing spoke for itself.
(Approaching Dusk)

CONTENTS

Approaching Dusk	10
Blake/London/Blake	12
Singing At Stars	20
The Easter Ballad	23
Dante/Brugge/Jerusalem	32
Dante	37
Essay On Beauty	41
Figures Of Zen	49

Night-songs:
    Themes and Variations Found
    in the Poems of St John of the Cross
	52

The Language Of Waves	73
To The House On Wheeler Hill	78
Yes	81

APPROACHING DUSK

APPROACHING DUSK

Approaching dusk the shadows danced
among and beyond themselves
and because it was Flanders
somewhere there was a ringing bell.
He could imagine how, beyond his window,
shadows approached then consumed the light,
how there would be those who would watch
and those who would not. Cyclists went by,
one had a light, one had not,
the clock seemed to miss every second beat.
Everything was possible –ambition, detachment,
both could be perfected in the instant of choosing,
the one would equal or cancel the other.
Yes, night was sacred, to those who believed
and to those who did not. Poetry?
that was the voice which did not interfere
with how each thing spoke for itself.

BLAKE/LONDON/BLAKE

BLAKE/LONDON/BLAKE

London, hidden London, his London
And sweet Thames flow softly
Flow onto/into words that are a key to the city
Flow forward into history from out of the mythos
Flow and flow
Sing and lull me to singing
As it was in the beginning
As it is in the tide's under-current and flow
– and songs flowing there –
Time and time
His and mine
Here in this room
The light beyond and the music of traffic and the deeper music of the world
Ends await but I cannot see them
Beginnings are far from here yet this is also a beginning
Unreal but so real city of the world
Your song the water's drive to the sea
And the sea, the sea, waiting and waiting as I also wait
So flow river flow
Flow back into sacred memory as you are prone to do and teach me that singing
Flow back into that voice I honour here

But who and what can name him in this time?
Unreal/twilight time of the world's changing in spite of his unchanging voice
Can I name, can I honour, can I outline his voice?
– poetry's prayer –
Hearing it here in the twilight
In London, sweet London
Here and now, there and then
As if it also was a Jerusalem
Secular and sweet to the eye
Even so, even so, his voice ringing in the bells of evening and the rush – bound traffic

Yes, his voice
This place
As he saw it more than what it is
Which is what I respond to
Reading him this twilight by the window in the first lights on the streets
Calling to him, saying yes and yes
Saying Yes to all that he saw and spoke
Of this place and that other
– the footprints visible yet –
Sweet London in that it was his
Still is
London deeper that the twilight and traffic
Where Jerusalem nests
Where the strings unwinds and history unwinds from a golden spool
– these words taken from what he gave –
To end – if it ends– in this twilight
In the first light of evening
In the echoes of his words upon this page

And flow river flow, flow to the sea
Flow river flow to the sea

Yet now in our time
– twilight in and of the world –
In our own voice
In what the eye sees of despair and beauty as they co-exist in the world
of evening
In the words that are spoken
In the words that form upon the page the prayers of the heart
Casting off –as he insists we should– the not human
Singing and singing
Of those cities and landscapes of the mind
Now in our time
In the world as it is
The beast unloosed and history waiting
The spool winding back all threads to itself
The city exposing the city it conceals

And language, language, language
Words on the page, in the mouth, and where else?
What but these words?
Where but this place?
When if not now?
Yes, now in our time
At this window and elsewhere
His words and those of every dancing master
– name them for yourself –
And the mills still churning
And those feet taking their first steps
And London waiting and waiting as I am waiting here by this window at twilight
His words a consolation – as poetry is and always is *'strong enough to help'*
There where hell and heaven open
To night
To each one
Wanted or not wanted hell and heaven open and at such moments who can say which is which?
Not I in this twilight
Not I reading his words by this window as the river still flows and the music ascends and the heart finds consolation to endure and endure
It was always so
It always will be
Blake still walking London as the heart sees it
As the eye delights in it
As the voice rises to song
Sing then the befitting song that you have known
The one in the heart's core
The one that motivates the voice to singing

Twilight and dark and the noise of the world
The shadows lengthen and the music grows wild as if it was sung in Darfur
London, London, flow river flow
This is the heart enduring

And the river dreams the city to the life that it will lead

The river his river
The dream his dream
Jerusalem stirring in all the cities of the world
In Baghdad and Darfur
Here and elsewhere and all the unmentioned cities of the heart
As music stirs, as numbers stir to perfect combinations
His words a shaping force
In London, in Lambeth
In Flanders where I live
In this twilight as I read by the first evening lights and the noise of the streets
To bear witness
To bear witness to the beast and the law
To sing, to affirm, to not hesitate – this is the requirement
Casting off the not human and merging into the imagination as he defined it
Yes and yes and yes again
All things in affirmation and joy and the heart singing them
As it sings in these lines
These lines and those others as a debt repaid and willingly repaid
Nothing escaping the eye's instrument nor the voice as it lauds
Yes, here, in this city as he has sung and decried it
Yet also sang to its betterment
London, this London
Unreal/real city of finance and men and the dead in their numbers
crossing that bridge
Hell at the gate of heaven – and nowhere else
As he sung them in extraordinary lines
Lines I read and am comforted by in this twilight
The myth and the story
The splendour and mire they issues from
In this London or elsewhere
In Flanders or Ireland or Venice
– I have loved these place with varying degrees –
Cities of the heart as that heart struggles to sing and to dance
As he encourages it
As Jerusalem shapes itself within the womb of the word and shakes the world
Yes, in this place

At this window in London
His London – but my London?
Only in the ways he has named and given form to
Only in his words
Only in the world as he defines it
Otherwise all is strange and profane and I cannot sing
– That song is one I do not know, the words are composed to a strange tense –
Yet I would sing
Of the river and city and his voice shaping them
Flow river flow, flow to the sea, and bear us all upon you
Flow to the cities of the heart and bring us home again
Flow river flow – he has named you
As I name him in these lines with joy and come to know something of his wild delight
Flow river flow – I name you also
And sing the child in its cradle
Yes, even in winter this must be sung
Now more than ever
In this place and not elsewhere
This London and the dead crossing the bridge in their numbers and the living moving between them
Yes, it is so
All things conspire as he conspires to utter a sacred word to the profane noise of the world

Lights in the evening dark
Lights on the traffic that passes
On the pages of the book I read from
His words driving the twilight towards the conclusions of night
And night comes
Darkness and darkness and the lights of the traffic
The page no longer visible but the words still thrilling
Ringing in the London dark – London and beyond
Listening at this window when I can no longer read
– now the world is truly hidden –
Unreal and real
Now in this time

Here in this place
Night-shadows moving across the bridges of the world
Then silence and silence as if some point of stillness had been reached
Darkness and darkness – the shadows weave the world of their making
yet the river still flows into history
The tides active underground and history stirring there
As if the darkness was something foretold
As if it was always bound to come to this
As if the night was as necessary to morning as this winter is to spring
And so the double-darkness comes
His words go on and language rises to the lips
Yes in the winter, yes in the dark, yes the word it reaches for
In our time
In this place
This place and beyond and everywhere inherent in this place
Flow river flow
Even in darkness the tides are beautiful and necessary
But to see beyond the darkness
To outwit the tide of the moment –
Yes, this is what he asks
This is what his words bend towards and I cannot deny them
Tides and cross-currents in the darkness of the world
And voices in that tidal dark calling for mercy and attention
For a voice that offer comfort
For a voice that will redeem them
– terror beginning where beauty ends –
But who will speak as he spoke?
Who sees the flaming core he drew his substance from?
The world grows cold in the darkness
Night shadows move through the kingdom of night
The night becomes the other of the day
And still the river flows
And still his words echo through the dark
Echo and echo – the same truths told of the city and the river
A voice redeeming the night from its darkness
The river flowing to the sea and the city come alive in the moonlight

Yes London, this London
Moonlight upon the roof of the world and his voice ringing there
Cast off, it calls, cast off!
Cast off the filthy rags! Cast off!
Cast off the destroyers of Jerusalem!
Yes, to do so in this moonlight after twilight
To do so in this city and all others
To wash the mind in the river that flows to the sea and to rise refreshed
To sing as he sung
To see London hidden in London
Then seeing it in moonlight as his voice rises again
His voice sprung from and returning to that core
Terror and beauty, terror and beauty
– one fading, one continuing –
The city casting off its filthy rags and the child crying in December
Yes and yes
To this and all things as he saw them
Voicing them now to the darkness of the world, the darkness and moonlight
Yes in the darkness, Yes in the moonlight
London his London
Visions that give the night its substance and music
And the voice singing that
Here in this time, here in this place and history happening everywhere
Unreal/real city
– the bridges empty and the busses running late –
Seen from this window in this moonlight
Sung for and sung for again and again
Outlined in these lines, embraced and defended
Vision's outline, vision's core

The stars go on and on and on
The stars go on and on

SINGING AT STARS

SINGING AT STARS

Not done. Not with full voice on clear frosty
    nights
nor with a pose suggesting benediction and
    blessing.
No, not done, but approved of and responded to
    When
found in a poem in which such things were done
    and done
to good intent. And at once it's familiar.
    As if
this was an art long practiced and indulged in.
    As if
singing with the voice alert to all the nuances
    of light
was some nightly ritual by one who does not believe
    in rituals.
As if the stars required it. As if by being
    such singing
was necessary to affirm something permanent in
    the flow
of time the stars observed. So I will sing now
    not hum
but sing as passionate as one is when in love. I'll go
    out
to the yard, assume a stance, and when the stars appear
    sing
as if song were sufficient praise for their being.

Not done,
no, not yet, but already the act is familiar to me
    who
has been a believer without the accurate means of praise
    but who
now find this to be an obvious act. Praise that it is!
    Praise
that it should be so! Praise for such glory on a night
    like this
when one wakes to the mode appropriate to stars
    and standing
there in a jubilant pose sings and sings and sings!

THE EASTER BALLAD

THE EASTER BALLAD

1

How not live it – that life – the one proposed by those verbs and words which take their élan from beauty?
How find it in the shambles of the world?
It will find you
The verbs will come and the words will flow and beauty is, as they say, unavoidable
You will be privy to what it has to offer
You will be servant and it will be master in a situation where to serve is the soul's delight and joy and purpose
Yes, even in our time, in the shambles of the world, such things are possible

And I have had dreams which were pleasing and wholesome and true
The spirit rose flushed as a snipe and took to the wind that bore it
There was joy abundant in the words as they came and the dreams fulfilled my expectations of them
Yes, in our time
In the world that this is – but the world as it truly is
Yes, beauty and beauty and no end to it
The pleasing dream, the pleasing verb
Words taking off on the freshest wind and the soul rising with them
Yes, how not live that life?
How refuse what it brings into the world?
There where the stars go on and on
There where the stars go on

Midnight, midnight, and the rose – and history not complete without it
There in auroral, splendid dark that hint of suns
Who would not see it as it shines in the dark and who will not celebrate it?
Sing '*I will*' to the dark and light
Learn the language of shadows
Probe the deepest pools of tradition and emerge into the freshening wind at dawn that rises and calls the soul to it
Yes, the soul and nothing less

The surge and celebration
The affirmation and the joy
And the wind lifting you higher and higher and higher!
Yes, I have dreamt and lived that life and relive it in these lines written for your sake – your sake and mine
Words on the wind, the soul like a snipe, the stars fading in the crispness of dawn
Why should I sing less?
Even midnight is beautiful and calming
That auroral dark to which I have given allegiance
For which I have sung all things and offered all verbs
And you – you will listen?
You will join with me in this song of praise?
Then sing me creation as Caedmon sung it in that verse
As I have sung it elsewhere and here
As it has prompted the verbs to form the words of affirmation
At midnight and near it
Singing for the rose
Singing and singing and no end to it
– I have said this before and will say it again –
As I work in the scriptorium or briar
As I walk these streets feeling that I am walking in Jerusalem
And I am
O yes, it is always to sacred cities that we go
Ithaca and Jerusalem
– I have sung this also and will sing it again –
No matter what the shadows conspired or language veered away from for there was always the rose at midnight

And here is the rose
Splendid and beautiful in a world that is beautiful but frequently sordid
Even so, even so, to sing at midnight and near it
To sing of the rose
To affirm in darkness the ascendancy of light
To respond to the wind at the dawn

To shape language accordingly
And always, always, the rose at the heart of all things
Midnight and midnight
The verbs and the vowels
The splendid darkness, the life-giving light
The voice faithful to both

So how not live it – that life in all its beauty?
Who will refuse the rose and its intentions?
Not I, not I, in this lifting wind
Not I at midnight and near it

2

Beauty and dreams, beauty and dreams, the heart sings and sings
To touch, albeit but once, the core of the rose
To sing the perfect verb and have that verb deliver the perfect lyric
– In April such things are possible –
April, April, yes, the heart knows it and sings

Beauty and dreams, beauty and dreams – this much is true, the rest is supposition
Whatever was forgotten is now remembered and celebrated
The rose makes its first tentative moves towards fullness and seeing this the heart cries out in wild delight
That music is its celebration for it must celebrate
Even in moonlight all seems blessed and atoned
Even in moonlight all seems formed and forgiven and so the heart seeks out the perfect language
What is the verb for Easter?
What is it but the resurrection of all things on this the splendid earth?
It is for this that the heart seeks the perfect lyric and all its failures are beautiful
Yes, the heart has many ambitions and all of them aspire to poetry
Yes, the heart aspires to prolong the traditions and does this with the verbs of midnight and moonlight

But to sing that dawn – that's the better difficulty
To sing the resurrection of all things on this the splendid earth – it is for this that the heart longs
Easter, Easter, – what are its verbs and in what language may they be spoken?
Tell me then speak that language in all its elegance
Yes, the heart aspires
Consider the rose
Consider its elegance and aspiration
This is the heart's ambition
This is what the verbs reach towards at midnight and near it
Beauty and beauty, beauty and dreams, how not live what is known?
Nothing defiles the intention of the rose though the rose is often sullied and soiled
As it was in Auschwitz
As it is in Darfur and elsewhere
As it is in the exile's cry for Jerusalem
And yet to touch, albeit but once, the core of the rose
It is for this that the heart sings in December and April
It is for this that it stirs the pools of tradition
And so language rises at dawn but what are the verbs and vowels of sunrise?
What are the words which will tell of the rose and the splendid dawn of Easter?
Therefore one beautiful failure after another
Language faltering at that threshold
Even so, even so
That much is beautiful in the shambles of the world and at least the rose is indicated
So much, so much, beauty and beauty – how will the heart sing it all?
It can and it can't
It falters and rises and falters again but always, always that singing
As there was that April in Greece
'Christ is risen! Christ is risen!' and who is there that would doubt it?
The world moving towards epiphany

Towards the beauty of the perfect word
Towards the rose and its core
And singing, singing, singing
Yes, the heart remembers
Remembers and longs and sings from memory and longing
Verb after verb, word after faithful word
The soul rising
The mind in wild delight
And all the verbs conspiring to utter a single word of praise
I have not forgotten nor will I forget
That word warms the mind and the mind is comforted

Beauty and dreams, beauty and dreams – this is the heart's condition
Beauty and dreams, beauty and dreams – this is the heart's longing in
April

3
To reconcile history to the rose
The blood on the stones and the exile's cry
The terror – and no beauty following
In Ithaca and Jerusalem
The rose profaned and condemned again, again
The bitter herbs and the exile's cry
And lostness reigning on the cities of the world
No, the heart cannot escape it
The eye cannot fail to see the evidence everywhere

Laments at midnight and near it
All seems moonless and dark
A weird music wails over the roofs of the world and all seem to know
that music
Only a Dante could sing it but only the rose can redeem it
Lostness, lostness, darkness and dark – a chill wind rises through the
night
Lament after lament

The pools empty and the voice stuck in the throat
And no escape nor let up in the winter
The heart broken, the soul shattered on the loom of time
Who now will sing for beauty in the world?

Midnight, midnight, stroke of a bell
Who sings for beauty in the world and who will forgive the history of the word?
The rose holds itself in the dark
The voices of praise are silent
Nothing seems atoned and all seems condemned
Darkness and darkness, darkness and dark
And were it not for the wailing there would be a bitter silence
Footsteps in fog – feet stagger in narrow lanes
Laments and wailing
A broken language – but the longing has not abated

And will the rose atone for history?
And will the rose silence the wailing of the world?
All seems to pass in silence into silence
And the dark seems neither auroral nor bright

Even so, even so
To sing at midnight and near it
To say that there in the dark the first light appears
To affirm the rose in the face of history
To acknowledge the dark without denying the rose
To sing a brother's lament and then to sing of the rose
To wash the stones of their blood
To cleanse the harbours of Ithaca and Jerusalem
To bring all things to the eve of Easter
To lay the wailing of the world at the stem of the rose
To wash all things in cleansing waters and not those waters the exile sings of
Yes, the wailing, darkness, and lostness
To bring these to the beauty of the rose

To sing with the exile then to carry him home – this is the heart's intent

4
And Christ the rose of history and history the history of the rose
All beauty bows down to the beauty of the rose

5
Ah yes, the sweetness of it – the affirmations of April and the heart's wild delight
How not live and celebrate it?
Night songs, dawn songs, words in the mouth – yes, these are the affirmations of April and the earth edging towards Easter
Holy, Holy, Holy, all things sing *Holy, Holy, Holy*
And here in this house in Flanders I also sing glory to all things
Holy, Holy, Holy – y es, this is the heart's cry and it wants no other
Neither in April nor December but especially in April
All things bending towards beauty and beauty bending towards the rose
The rose of history and the rose that resides outside of time and they are one
Beauty, beauty, all things moving towards beauty
So how not live that life and celebrate it?
Who would refuse the rose in April?
April – death – O sweetness – and resurrection
And the heart wanting more and language struggling to name it
The verbs laced with affirmation, the vowels also
Language rising like a bird that breaks cover at dawn
And the soul hovering and thrilled at the beauty of the world
Holy, Holy, Holy – what else is there to sing
What other songs can be heard in April?
What else but the rose gives meaning to time?
Who will sing in April what he sings in December and who will refute the one or the other?
December, December, the earth yields its promise
April, April, the earth yields again
And I have sung at both seasons – through winter dark and ice on the rose

And what did I sing but what memory knows of December turning to April
Yes, all things, all things, all things bow down to the rose
Moving out of history into wonderment
Singing and singing for joy at love's pageant in April
And the pools of tradition stirring
And the air winnowed and clean
And language rising to meet the beauty of the rose
Yes, this is April – April and beyond it
Easter of the world, Easter of the heart
The heart singing its affirmation in ballads of praise
The rose flourishing by the trellis on the wall
The rose flourishing in the fire of the mind
Within and without time
And Easter moving towards the solstice
And the earth in its language of praise and celebration
Here on this earth, here on this earth
All things moving towards praise and celebration in that love *"that moves the sun and all the stars*

DANTE/BRUGGE/JERUSALEM

DANTE/BRUGGE/JERUSALEM

City and city – walking at night – but who/where am I?
Echo and song, echo and song – the world sleeps and dreams
Night-time in the cities of the heart – which is Brugge and which is Jerusalem?
Jerusalem you are as beautiful as Blake described – as beautiful but as bitter
The exile sings at your gate
The stones are covered in blood
The lanes of Brugge and Jerusalem converge and I cannot tell one from the other
It was always so and it always will be
Mirror, converse image where language roots and stems from in words that are holy and profane
The shadows uniting and telling a story
The one I unravel in this fashion
Brugge and that Other and the one walking there – the one who knows their singing
As I would know and be him unravelling the knots of confusion and silence
Singing also
In these lines and in whatever can be sung and no end, no end to it
Dante, Dante, – teach me those verbs
Let all the words of winter bow to the verbs of spring and may it be spring in the city
Let these also be the verbs of April
April and spring
Hope in the heart and hope in the world and voices raised in singing
Yes, all things for this
Hope and whatever the heart endures
Like music outlasting the notes on the page
The heart singing wildly and wildly
Twilight – yet with clarity for whatever the heart endures – and singing, singing for that
It was always so and always will be

Music and no end to it – nor to the longing it gives voice to
Longing that names the heart in its endurance
Longing that says *'Remember me, remember me'*
Those words a motif and motive
Here and now in the world

And will you walk beside me as I go?
Will you also sing down the alabaster halls of silence and night?
And there will be no end to it?
No point at the which the song will finish though it will hesitate
No word be it holy or profane that cannot be used and uttered
So walk with me down the lanes of this town and tell me where we walk

Jerusalem, Jerusalem, you are the heart's legacy, Dante the singer, and Brugge in the twilight of evening
Evening of the world
Evening in which these psalms rise and are offered to beauty wherever it is found and celebrated
Here and now, there and then, and Dante at the tiller of the little skiff of verse
Yes, to beauty, to beauty, all things for beauty
Walking these streets – but walking where?
The streets of affirmation turning into the streets of passion
Blood on the stones
House after house
And a bitter wailing rising over the roofs of the world
This is also the heart's legacy
This is what it sings through winter 'till April
Enduring and wailing – even to the beauty of the world and complaints raised against it
And there seems no resurrection for the crushed heart
All seems bitter and empty and only a Dante could sing it
And I cry for the pain of Jerusalem
Yet beauty remains – and this is also the heart's legacy
Wailing and beauty commingling on these streets

But Brugge or Jerusalem – I cannot say
And there is much that I cannot say yet the heart will attempt all things
So whose is that hand upon the tiller and who does the singing?
Where do I walk and what does it matter?
These streets merge into those small lanes and those forms assume their shadows here therefore Dante teach me the difference or teach me how they are one and the same as twilight closes about the streets and I do not know their names
Jerusalem, Jerusalem, the heart longs and longs
It sings for beauty at twilight – at twilight and the coming dark
For beauty, all things for beauty
Psalm after psalm
In whatever language of the heart that it is sung
In Brugge or in Jerusalem
In the city they merge into and formed
In the uncalm longings of the heart

Dante –Brugge– Jerusalem – this is the triad of night
Shadows weave a language I must speak
Darkness that could be the auroral darkness of God –whose hand now upon the tiller?– and the splendid darkness of the river
Flow river, flow, out of forgetfulness and into remembrance
Flow river, flow
The world is uneasy and no bird flies
Silence and silence and then the ringing of a bell
Midnight in Brugge and Jerusalem
Midnight on all the cities of the world and the exile crying in his longing
Who will cry with the exile?
Who will sing what he sings and weep what he weeps?
I sing with herbs and honey in my mouth
I am also that exile, I am also that song, I am also his lostness in the world
Exile and music
Exile no matter where the heart walks and music no matter the silence

And it is this that the heart endures – exile and music and whatever can be sung and calling on Dante to sing it
In Brugge as in Jerusalem
In gracious and intricate verse
In the perfect modulations of the heart
Teach me that music
Let me sing Jerusalem and let me sing Brugge
Let me walk in this darkness to a known destination
Call it the core, or the heart's verb, or something that is neither and both
The fire in the mind that burns all names and leaves only the unsinged core
Burned like the heart is
Burned to scattered ash and perfect silence
There where all names merge
Where the exile can truly sing
Where the blood is washed from the stones
Where two cities merge to form a third – or expose the one at the common core
Where perfect silence is
Where words form the perfect alliance
Words that can be sung from midnight 'till April and to which the exile can respond

Yes, for this and no less
For this and all things in the dark
For this and exile and music
There where all the shadows bow down
There where the stars go on and on, there where the stars go on

DANTE

DANTE

and the traffic spurts
to the next stop or go,
as motorists rage against the wait
of two seconds more
even though
and although deeply unconcerned
this is where history happens

Darkness zooming towards the light.
The air chilling by full degrees.
Everything heavy under its own weight
though nothing, nothing had changed.

The city was itself if itself gone strange,
become less actual place,
more a soul's geography
where from distance and nearness
signal and counter signal spoke
of an underpinning reality
equally imagined as reality or fable,
but where, as I looked upon it
death alone seemed living master;
where even though I had known it
I had not thought death had undone
so many yet it had – for there they were:
functional but without cadence,
interchangeable shades,
incidental even to themselves
so lost in their functions were they.

They walked and I watched;
my eyes narrowing
as a tailor squints through
his needle's eye, for it was fate,
not curiosity, which led me there
to see the familiar gone strange and profane.
But you need no words of mine
to name the plight of those who sang
attempting to sing

who lacked both words and pitch.
It was as if they lay in a ditch
writhing for the love of that place
which is our common homeland
without which
all is death's sly won realm
the song of which is little more than moaning

If I tell you this and it grieves you
know   what I intend by this.
Root from your soul such customs
as make you love the dark
you cannot plumb.
Know who it is who tells you this
and why
and know that you should listen as I sing.

For these words and what they signify
are true; compared to which
others will seem like burnt-out coal.
And if I tell this right
all will shift as I report what has been willed
and all will move towards harmony
and you will not miss your glorious arrival
if the word will be the mirror of the thing.
For even there in that place
much can be won
by who is prepared to try his living luck.

Darkness zoomed but the good light held
as I prepared to walk there,
not as one new come to that estate
nor once there to despise them.
I was making for the river
led by what I remembered
and by what I moved towards
which even those I moved amongst
moved also – all be it by loss
while I drew close to all that apprehended good

– self evident, not 'demonstrated' –
to which I was both open and exposed.

It was as though a star had changed location
and so re-lit the world.
For there, where the strings were loosed
and motion whirled to a senseless stop,
all was set to sudden dancing
though every part was where it always was!
The world was still the familiar one
where, if much was shabby,
much was blatantly misunderstood
when the eye
guided by the surface sense of things
ignored its core quiddity.

(Shelley saw such as this inherent in
and central to the making act,
having seen in advancing spring
that rightful ascendancy
making incites out of the ground its roots in,
vision the eye openly delights in
to renew the soul's cadence for self's delight.)

And there it was, the world,
starlit more than stars could light
to a potency no dark could usurp,
as if necessity was the cause of this effect!
Call it experience, vision, art,
and if your imagination cannot run
to heights like these to trace this
to the ground it roots in – remember this:
no seed thrives in unwelcoming ground
nor thrives when at odds with time and place.

What I saw – I saw
and quickly followed where it led.
Glimpsed the river's brightening sheen,
watched for the dawn star's imminent rise.

ESSAY ON BEAUTY

ESSAY ON BEAUTY

"The soul should always stand ajar, ready to welcome the ecstatic experience."
                                                Emily Dickinson

Beauty, beauty, I have longed for it under the stars
Even in November & its aftermath
The naked trees & the birdless skies
& the longing of the heart for the fullness of summer
Have been, & am, the acolyte of its devotions
And not at all reluctant but eager, keen, adamant, sure
As if I knew it in all its forms
As if the voice was raised in praise of that
As if there was nothing else to sing

Nightly, walking these streets in moonlight
Uttering my praise as if crazed by the moon
Reading the shadows as if they were the language of night & poetry a consolation
Even in the rains that comfort & heal the fractured heart
Embracing that & the language of shadows
Learning to speak the language of night as part of the language of beauty but never satisfied
The heart never so sated that it cannot take more
The mind crying out in delight

& the quietness of the water in moonlight
The lake a mirror of moonlight & clouds in which I see the beauty of the sky
Singing for that
In these lines & those others until I am voiceless & silent & in silence praising also
Proficient in all the ways I need to be yet it is never enough
Beauty defying me at every turn & history my witness
Book after book
– we are Dante's children in the world's twilight –

The language of memory & the language of forgetfulness & the language of love
All the voices of praise in November
And unpremeditated prayer rising to the lips & then uttered to the night
Here in this place as if it were all places –& it is
Where I sing what is permitted me
Where the heart bows down and says this is the place of adoration
& the stars in their manyness
As if all the world had come to this place
The heart drifting in wonderment & no end to it
Here in the world I love but have no befitting music for
Seeking in moonlight on water the appropriate voice
The one that speaks to this time & place but also to the timeless & the placeless
For beauty's sake
Singing in no name but my own yet singing for all names
This night & all others & in daytime's language of all is that is visible as beauty always is
Even in the language of absence
Even in November & its birdless skies
Especially in this place & this time
Here
Where history happens
Beauty of winter & its necessity
– I am also leafless –
& the moonlight on the rooftops of this town
Memory forgetting nothing
Neither the bird nor the leaf nor the song that drives the summer
Repeating it again & again
Each time a new beginning, a new failure to fully hold it yet loving such failures

As if, this once, the heart might know it all & the voice express it
Night-walker though shadows under the clouds
Saying each time *Here it is, Here it is*
Then falling into the shadows

ESSAY ON BEAUTY

My footsteps & these words across the rooftops of this town
My Brugge
As if it were an entrance or an example
& the echoes of these streets at midnight
As if I had come to a long-desired place
Half-content to have uttered some praise or at least to indicate it
To say – here, here is where it resides as it also reside wherever you are
& the leafless, birdless trees in their naked beauty
Prone to history yet longing for the beautiful
Finding hints & revelations
Guiding the heart & the mind by them
Singing for you as I sing for myself
A comfort, a duty
Falling in love with the moonlight again
Looking for the bird who will fly in the night
– beauty, you understand, is capable of such things –
& the bird of the heart fluttering in its cage
Here am I, Here am I, it cries out
Content to admit its failures but not so content that it will cease
In this moonlight or some other
Prying into water to see the beauty there
Seeing so much but singing so little for so little can be sung

Beauty is never enough nor what I can sing of it
Here in moonlight by the winter lake
Shall I sing the voices of the night which whispers across the rooftops of the world?
I shall do all this & more but it will not be enough
The heart is never satisfied & beauty is never sung in its fullness
Its hunger for music unappeased & always will be
& beauty urging it on to seek more & more
The moonlight an evidence, the shadows an invitation, the lake a testimony
But restless, restless, restless, restless
No, I am not satisfied nor will be
Beauty defying the nets I place about it

My language composed of a few broken words – yet with what else can
I sing?
Answer me if you can, remain silent if you can't
Only beauty satisfies the heart
Only beauty ever has though I have known so little & so much
– sometimes the mind has been fickle in its allegiance –
& every site a Temenos
Holy!, Holy!, Holy! cries the heart –& the mind concurs
What the eye sees the heart sings out
Longing for it under the stars in these my devotions
Remembering Keats – how could I not? –
Poetry my refuge –the art the heart taking a consolation in these lines
and those others & not at all reluctant
Sigh after sigh in this moonlight
Vagabond, lost, delighting in that
Time's fool & not caring
Uttering my praises as if crazed by the moon
In the rains that comfort & heal the fractured heart
& history has no function there nor prerogative
The fractured heart bowing down & uttering its adorations
November, November, soon it will be the solstice
& what might the heart sing at mid-winter's fire?
Beauty of winter & the stars in their manyness
As if this was the place of the world's end or beginning though there is
no beginning & the heart sees no end to beauty
& the script of the shadows there for the learning
To learn that language – yes, to let the heart comfort itself with those
verbs
& the necessity, the accuracy of silence

I have sung for nothing else
Neither in this moonlight nor in daytime's surge
Even when the heart had no words to sing out it still sang *Holy!, Holy!,
Holy!*
I have nothing else to sing so I will sing this one song again & again
& the stars will be my witness & the water will listen

& the shadows will tell me what I do not know
& I will tell you that here in these lines
In November until April

Ah Keats, you come to mind
You with your one concern which is my concern
In Rome and/or in Brugge
Yes, beauty my one concern
I have sung for nothing else nor will I sing without it
& moonlight giving its accuracy and rightful moment
All sites merging into this site & its acropolis of shadows
Beauty, beauty, yes, the heart lurches towards it & no other
Beauty in the stillness of the lake
Language beginning where language ends
& the heart inflamed by the moonlight

It was always so, it always will be
This is where the heart finds a first consolation though the heart is never consoled
Perhaps appeased – for one moment at least but not in its hunger for beauty
Ah yes, Keats, you knew that
You wrote each line from that perspective
I write from the perspective of this lake in moonlight

& still the heart sighs in its longing
Fractured but longing for healing
Appeased for the moment but not fully appeased
Beauty – & no end to it nor to the heart's longing
Nor language enough to speak all its names nor silence enough to bless it
I have sung for this where even the silence was part of the song
& not even one fraction fully told
No, but attempted
The heart sighing again & again on the electric air
November – but that does not matter
Nor even mid-winter's fire

Nothing matters except that beauty be & be sung

& do you listen there where you are?
Do you also walk the midnight streets in moonlight?
Tell me if you do, tell me if your don't, & let us sing this song together

I have sung for nothing else
The heart has endured & the mouth has exposed all things, all things for its sake
O the heart is crazed by the moon & cannot be silent neither in these lines or some other
Moonlight, moonlight, a sigh & a sigh
Beauty & nothing else
Keats would agree
What is it he says? Ah yes: *and evenings steep'ed in honeyed indolence*
There where the moon is reflected in water
There where the clouds pass in the mirror
So compose the language of the poem from that
In November until April
& then beyond that into the blaze of high summer when the frost is forgotten
When the lakes moves with the first summer winds
When language stirs again & again & again

The heart is a rose opening to mid-winter's fire
Nothing, nothing has been forgotten
The rose repeats itself upon the trellis on the wall
Moonlight repeats itself upon the lake the swans will move out on in morning
& beauty despised in our time, denied by our language
Even so I sing –my failures perhaps, even so, I sing for the beauty of the rose repeating itself by the wall
For the heart in its fractured self
& the moonlight & the clouds
Beauty, and no end to it
& the healing of the fractured heart
& nothing matters except that beauty be sung

ESSAY ON BEAUTY

As Keats would have us do – as would every dancing master
The hands own weaving!
Tracing his substantial signature, easing into the rightness of his lines
especially in November
Acolyte to its devotions
The heart surrendering to beauty & all that it blesses blessing as it does
the rose repeating itself on the trellis on the wall
Repeating myself so as to say a simple thing
That beauty is, was and will be
In these lines & all others –mine & yours
Nothing equalling this satisfaction
Neither language nor love if they be cast without it
Language returning to its first root
& the roots deep in the beauty of the world as I see it
Here where the lake receives the moon & the moon receives the
fractured heart
Yes, all things for beauty's sake
Even in November & its aftermath
& the fire in the heart & the fire in the mind
Learning to speak the language of night as part of the language of
beauty
The shadows & the clouds & the language of both
The heart never satisfied no more than the tongue is
Proficient in all the ways I need to be yet it is never enough nor can ever
be
Beauty is endless, the longing also
Even in November & its aftermath
& history my witness
Dante's child, his & no others'
Where the moon upon the lake is the language of night
Where all things merge & I sing & I sing
Where all things merge under this glitter of moonlight & stars

FIGURES OF ZEN

FIGURES OF ZEN

On a whim –or sparked by inspiration's charge? –
on a glorious day we drove to the sea.
You held the car steady at a flawless ninety an hour
in a motion that was so perfect I had credence in it
& did not disturb you by talking. To have done so
would have been a lack of faith in the motion
with which you drove us through a familiar landscape,
in which I did not know if your skill was one of attention
or letting go but content that the outcome would be
all we wanted it to be; something I relaxed into
until we came to the beach & saw those statues in the sea,
those figures of Zen standing passive, silent, open eyed,
set in the sand which shifted underneath their feet
the tide made wet & dogs pissed on
then moved away indifferently from though I was not indifferent.
It was as if Easter Island had come to our Flemish shore,
as if the mysteries had entered ordinary lives –& they had –
in an artists' realisation of stillness & motion, of distance & nearness,
of the unsteady borders between the marvellous
& the everyday; a zone we had travelled into when in truth
we had travelled nowhere beyond the motif of the day.
We also faced the same horizon, we also stood between two elements
& surely for some onlooker we were also statues in the sand
suggesting much but offering no conclusions.
If conclusions existed they existed beyond the horizon
& what can I tell of distance & nearness & stillness & motion
that you might know of by reading this?

FIGURES OF ZEN

You said that letting go was the motion I needed to understand
what was at work here, so again I was the passenger
of your direction & pace,
receiving instruction, being inducted into the rites of bronze,
the intentions of stillness, the many silences' you said I should listen to
& the fluctuations of the horizon as the tide came in & in.
What moves us to that which is beyond ourselves?
What do we answer the horizon with?
Whatever it is it was active then and still is
in the memory by which these lines are written

NIGHT-SONGS:
(Themes and Variations Found in the Poems of St John of the Cross)

NIGHT-SONGS:
(Themes and Variations Found in the Poems of St John of the Cross)

Ignoring the created
Remembering the creator
Vision set on the inner
Vision of love that is greater

*

Night-time, night-time
Beauty and dreams
The soul longs and longs

To sing what it has surrendered to
To sing what it loves and loves –
Yes, this is poetry, all else is prose
And the word is the word is the word

Night-time, night-time
Beauty and dreams
And the heart wandering in gardens

Night-time, night-time
Echo and song
What is there that cannot be sung?

Tell me, tell me
For I want to know
In this night of silence and stars

If I were Dante
If I had that voice
If I knew the language that lovers know
But I only know poverty

Then take my poverty
O You, blessed One
Take it and mend it or break it!
Night-time, night-time

Beauty and dreams
The soul walks in a garden

And there is no darkness it has not known
Nor isolation it has not surrendered to
Not even in the dust where it sought heart's desire

I sing and I sing
As all things sing
Music! Music!
Let there be song
Or that silence I'm more familiar with

Beauty and dreams
Beauty and dreams
This is the song of my longing

Here in night-time
Or at the dawn-season
Layla sought for
And Layla found
– O shimmering truth! –

And You are Layla
And always have been

Layla or Christ
What matter the name
When the heart shudders and shudders

Night-time, night-time
Beauty and dreams
This is the song of my longing

  *

*Divine Verb
The virgin's fruit ripens;
She walks now to your door
If you'll allow*

*

Beauty and dreams
Beauty and dreams –
I have known nothing else

Even when I denied
I truly affirmed

Consoled – even in night-time
Even in the darkness
There in the night

Singing and singing and no end to it
A foolish one to the ways of the world
But wise in this adoration

May it always be so
And may I always say

Rejoice, rejoice, rejoice with me
In this love we are both reflected
By mountain, stream or placeless place
We both pass undetected

*

O venture of delight!
In safety, in disguise
(O happy enterprise)
With no body else in sight
While the house slept

Upon that lucky night
In secrecy
(I was not susceptible to sight)
And with no other light
Then the light of my heart
I crept, I crept to your door

Up the stair, up the stair
Not seen by other eyes

I went without discerning
Any light other
Then the light burning in my heart

And that led me
Faithfully
To You
Whose love I knew
And no other love replaces

Night was my guide
Though it was night-time
Night joining lover to Bride
And the one becoming
The other

I will sing this again
And again
It is a story I will tell
For the rest of my life
Of all the gifts that were given

And I was past caring
My senses suspended
All longing ended but not ended
And no care other
Than the pleasure of the Bride

*

Who puts this song into my mouth?
It does not matter
But tell this to the chief of musicians –
That all must be sung for her sake
And for no-one, no-one else.

*

Dreams
Dreams and names
The heart yields and yields

Who would sing less
Or some other song
When there is the music of her name

Layla, Layla, sweetest Christ
All songs are turned towards you

    *

Where are you hiding?
You left me to moan
You left me with this wound
It is my dearest treasure

If you should see her
If you see her tell her
That in this absence I die
The second death of souls

I'll go to the mountain
I'll go to the stream
Surely I'll find her
And she will redeem

This lostness
This longing
This bridal-delight

This longing
All longing
In this darkest night

    *

Enough!
Send no messenger
But come as you are
Bring me what I long for

This cannot continue –
No, this absence must end
You have the arrow and you the bow

And I am wounded

Why did you pierce me
Only to leave again?
Tell me, tell me,
You should enjoy the plunder of your crime

So come, end my suffering
And send no other physician
You and only You
Can heal and mend and repair

*

Wounded, and wounded for love
I call on you –
Turn like the dove
Come to my branch and bower

And it is always night before dawn
Night in its silence and mystery
It is music without sound
The music that enamours

Come, the bed is ready
In the purple tent
And I wait impatiently
For your footstep, your call

I decorate the world for your coming
And sing a desolate song of absence
What else am I to do?
Until you come self is in mutiny

*

Beauty and dreams
Beauty and dreams
The heart longs for more

What can be said
And what can be sung

That I have not attempted?

I attempt all things
In beauty and dreams
And lay the prize at your feet

Answer me now
Answer me now —
If that is your pleasure

Even this absence is love
I am bridegroom and groom
I have and have not

I read the shadows
They are a language which says
'remember me, remember me'

And I have not forgotten
That even my infidelities
Are yours, are yours, are yours

Beauty and dreams
And a bridal delight
To what else have I been faithful?

To these, to these
And to whatever name
You choose to dress yourself in

Night is dark
Yet even the dark
Attests your sloe-eyed beauty

In darkness singing
Of absence and grief
You bring and shatter and mend

    *

That fountain —
Yes, I know it
Although it is night

Its source is a deathless spring
And I can guess that source
Even though it is night

Yet who can know its origin?
None can
And yet from that origin it arose
In the night

And nothing in this world is as beautiful
In the day
Or night

It is a river and you cannot tell its depth
Or find a way to cross it

Its clarity is that of pure water
And out of that
Comes the light by which we see
In the night

Believe me – that water rushes between the banks
And contain my heaven and my hell
In the night

Its current is not to be stopped nor altered
In its flow through
The night

And out of this a new current swells
Which nothing else can equal
In the night

This feeds the heart and gives it strength
In the night

Yes, it is night – but what of it?
The water flows from that fountain
And gives the earth its green and wholesome things

And all creatures draw sustenance there –
Though in the dark of day

Or night

That source is always hidden from our sight

*

And what can I give you
That you do not have?

Shall I come with song?
But you are the Singer

Shall I come with flowers
When you are the Rose?

Only this heart, only this heart
I have nothing but the humility it knows

*

Night-time, night-time
Songs in the dark
This is my one delight

Night-time, night-time
Beauty and dreams
I have nothing but this singing

*

Flame burns the soul to ash
And the soul is pleased —
Come bride, tear the robe!

In the killing is the life
And there are no debts or burdens

Ash and flame, heart's desire
Of living so as not to live
And dying so as not to die

*

And by what waters
Have I not wept —

Wept and been happy with tears

On alien ground
I sought her –
Even in dust, even in dust

Do not blame me for this –
I seek her where I must

Only this pain consoles me
Only this exile is home

Hope upon hope upon hope –
This is my longing

There by foreign streams
There in foreign lands

Dying and dying over and over
Yet living again and again

Come bride – unite us!
Tear the robe
Let all things be undone
– I don't care! –

Burn – and the world burns
And I am also ashes in the fire

It was always so and always will be –
Your word in this flesh is a wound

*

Dreams, dreams,
Beauty and dreams
The heart know exile and pain

It sings the one song
It tells the one story
It tells it again and again

Dreams, dreams
Beauty and dreams

Lover and beloved

Dreams, dreams
Beauty and dreams
The fire descends with the dove

  *

And the world betrays the beauty of the Rose
Lesser mirrors give back a lesser light
A trivial dance and a plastic flower
Hold the world entranced

Yet I have seen creation at its best
Earth by heaven blest
Divinity claiming a debt from earth
And the rose grew and flourished by the wall

  *

Running with hares
Hunting with hounds
In a willow grove
My true love was found

My true love was found
Dressed as a bride
The willow had driven
A shaft through her side

Berries of blood
Formed where she lay
In a cluster of berries
She peacefully lay

That evil willow
Sought her for harm
Sought her and found her
And caused love's alarm

But love's alarm
Can be love's delight

If berries are blood
So beautifully bright

I ate of those berries
So blood-red and warm
The berries would cancel
The willow's cruel harm

For running with hares
And hunting with hounds
Dressed in best bridal
My true love was found

*

*Daughters, daughters
Even as you behold the rose
Keep your distance
For this is a threshold
You may not cross*

*Consider the mountain
And stay hidden from view
My darling
But watch her retinue
Sail for strange islands*

*

*Ceaseless – in that strange place
The thoughts that came to me*

*Peace and piety interwove a net about
My heart*

*I was captive and joyous
And the solitude was profound*

*Wisdom was there but I will not say
What I heard or what I saw*

*As mystery after mystery
Tore down and rebuilt my thoughts*

I will be telling this over and over
Until I am old
And even then it will not be enough

To come to yourself you must shed your self
And every human disguise

Though the more I climbed
The less I understood
But joy still filled that place

Wisdom is a force that no man can wield
Nor change its course

So you pass beyond knowledge into that bliss
That is the wiser ignorance

If you would ask the essence
Then say
'It comes from the Divine Presence'
And let that be everything
You need to know –

The sudden sense of it overflowing
And mercy bestowing

Yes, that was it –
Mercy and light in that strange place

Where rapture told what words can never tell

    *

Tell it with a stone –
It hides among grain

Tell it with a word –
But each word is hollow

Tell it with a bone –
It hides in the marrow

Tell it with a bird –
The bird has gone

Tell it with a tree –
Only bark will remain

Tell it with a shell –
It sank in the sea

Tell it with a bow –
It has fled with the arrow

*

And it is true –
The heart has been fickle
The tongue has been faithless
Even so
I was thinking of you

And did you see me
As I ran
From place to place –
Intemperate with desire
Wild with longing?

Believe me
– And you know this to be true –
Even then
Even as I confessed to strange idols
I was thinking of you

Forgive then
Forgive the expectations
Which I raise
And walked according to
And believe me

Those expectations
Were raised by You!
That's right –
You are as much to blame in this
As I am

So let there be silence
Let there be love
Let their be forgiveness
For the heart
That has loved you too much

    *

Yes – the unexpected
The thing that I cannot foretell
Nor prepare for

Infinite joy
And the appetite for bliss –
I never tier of it
And never will
Even so, even so
The unexpected –
That which I cannot foretell
Nor dress for

For the heart is restless in this –
It is a journey
Which it never tires of
It runs and it is not weary
And uphill, uphill goes
In search of that which it
Cannot foretell
Nor dress for

Yet to have loved You
– and been pierced in the bargain –
Finds everything
Changed around
And health is sickness
And sickness health
And I ask for that
Which others deny

Do not be amazed at this
The pleasure of life
Turns bitter in separation
And that is the enemy
Of bliss
Yet then, even then,
It prepares for what it
Cannot foretell

Only love may steal a glance
At the Divine hand
Only love can answer the call
That love draws out –
It is for this
That it prepares
It is this that it expects

And nothing equals this charm –
Neither created nor creature
Not the bliss of the earth
And the joy of its song –
This and only this
Will satisfy me
In ways that are unexpected
Which I cannot tell

No, nothing delights
As that delights
Nothing calms the wayward heart
And herds it home
Nothing begot can give the joy
Which Joy alone brings
In unexpected ways

Yes – the unexpected
Something I cannot foretell
A theme that cannot be sung

*

There are the lovers and the Beloved
Each seeks the other
One step or a thousand unites them
Such steps the joy of lovers

*

Sweet Christ grant this –
An answer to my anguish and bliss

Accept that I have been profane
Accept that I will be again

Forgive my infidelity and let
Your love new joy, new joy beget

Love is the flame for which I yearn
Come touch me – let me burn!

*

For I have no love
Which would trap me
To bitterness
For I have you
My gentle Christ
And in this grove
I have shaped a hollow
Pine-needles for a bed
That in the morning
My cloak is full of

Among the mirth
Of singing birds
I carry my psalms
At my approach
They do not flutter
I know their song
They mine

May you hear it tonight
And answer
My gift-giving Christ

For I ask only this –
To continue here
Among the berries
The bushes and herbs
To have my soul
Rise up in praise
With the notes of birds
And know that to you
This is pleasing
I ask only this my Christ

*

Midnight, midnight, stroke of a bell, the world sleeps and sleeps
The world betrays the beauty of the rose
Rose, rose, rose of all my days and desires
The heart longing and longing and no end to it
Not in the night, not in the dawn, not in silence or song
Yet the dark would defile the rose
And so to sing and set the darkness ringing with delight at the rose
With the beauty of its core
With the beauty of its sepals
With the beauty of its colour and its form
Rose, rose, rose of all my days you are my one desire
And Christ the rose of history
The rose gathers all beauty to itself
Beauty and beauty
Beauty and dreams
At night and the dawn-season
History, history, you are also the rose and Christ the rose of history
Even in the dark
There where midnight rings with the stroke of a bell
Midnight, midnight, voices in the night

This voice, this voice
And all things for *Your* sake
You most beautiful and mild
You of the scorching glance
Whose mildness burns my heart and soul
And what is the soul but its longing?
And what is longing but song unsung?
I sing at midnight and near it
Here in the dark
Here with the memory of the rose and the name of Christ on my lips
All things for his sake
History and art and whatever is sung or is silent
And beauty preceding all things
Even at midnight
Even in the darkness of the world
Longing and longing and no end to it
– There never has been and there never will be –
The heart trafficking with whatever will show it beauty
All beauty a derivative of the rose
And the rose in its endless meanings and implications
History also – if it be rightly sung
History the child of the rose of Christ – who is history itself and its sweetness
Singing for that
At midnight or noon
Here in this room and here in the world
Singing at midnight and no end to it nor the longing
Singing and singing
One name repeated, one name espoused though all names bend to the rose
Beauty and longing, silence and song
In the world and in the Atomic Will
And history its aftermath
Here in the world at midnight and at morning's delight
Singing and singing and no end to it

Singing for beauty and its true silence
Singing for love o precious love
For the victory of the rose in its splendid pageant
There where the music is
There where the silence is
Where they meet and join and are one and are the spot I try to sing from
Yes, it is beauty and beauty and that beauty is Christ
It always has been and it always will be
Then forgive that I falter
That I fail and fail and falter again
Yet this is my longing so what can I do but sing and sing?
And you – have you listened?
Have you also sung your song to the rose?
Have you also said that history and the rose are one and that history is
the consequence of the rose?
Tell me, tell me
I will listen and sing with you or will sing alone
I will always sing alone
To the dark and the dawn
To the silence and song and have no care for the cost
Let ashes rage upon the world and the robe be torn – I don't care
Consequence is not my concern
Only song is
Only this song at midnight and near it
Only at the dawn
Only in history and Christ the rose of history

Yes, for this all things
Beauty and exile and always this singing
And always the rose at its core

Rose of the core
Rose of delight
I sing and sing and fall silent

All earth bows to the beauty of the rose.

THE LANGUAGE OF WAVES

THE LANGUAGE OF WAVES

1

There was the glittering clack of language on the tongue,
    words that told
their truths and evasions were marching over the laws
    of decorum
and propriety usurping every fallow verb and ploughing
    the ground
with the seeds of their own amazement. The rights of
    anyone
to walk and talk there were ignored. The words continued
    to be concerned
only with themselves. I was, of course, neither indifferent to
    nor unconcerned
by this. I also had my rights – but what were they and what
    strength
did they possess in such a situation? I was enamoured
    none the less
and charmed and followed where they led even if I did not
    recognise
the territory they were marching over. And that's the way
    it began,
the way the words marched ahead of themselves and insisted
    I follow
and I did – but would you believe me if I said that I knew
    nothing
of the outcome. It was as much a surprise to me as it will be
    to you
and that there are boundaries I know nothing of in advance.
    And this is the way
it happens every time, the pace that is followed, the tempo
    I attempt
to keep pace with – and which, succeeding or failing, write
    out
the results and find myself among this strange cadence.

2
Like the sea on the stones on a beach of stones and shells
    or the way
the marvellous words of moonlight shone out in the dark
    so they covered
the ground they spread themselves about. There was starlight
    in the dark –
this much I remember but what exactly the words drew their
    strength from
was something which even then eluded me. And so I moved in
    that ignorance
which was also a delight and to which I gave myself as one
    would
to one's lover – which is to say without reticence or hesitation
    though
let it be said I was also anxious for the outcome – not directing
    it
but following where it led until it leads to these words on this
    page
you hold in your hands and try to follow where I lead.

3
And where do I lead if not back into the cave of words as I
    know it
and attempt to shine a light on that dark which is life giving
    and naming?
Yes, this is what the mind bows to and accepts and says that
    it
is the true giver of wholesome light. Yes, words on the stones
    of the beach
I've walked so many times I am familiar with it even in the dark
    and also in
the sunrise which will come. Juan de la Cruz has also walked
    there
and knew it better than most – but this does not alarm me. I must

walk
in the dark that is particular to me and draw the words my tongue
    calls forth
and offers up to the sightless world. We each move in dark. The
    lighthouse flashes
its code and the darkness appears and reappears. And so the words
    come
out of that and I must catch them while I can as they glitter on the
    tongue
and offer their content and verve. Yes, the moonlight is all, the
    lighthouse
beyond is part of the beauty of night – the one that language moves
    towards
and from which it begins to sing the subtle praises of itself.

4
And as they clacked they told out a marvellous story which can
    be indicated
but not repeated: how each wave was in itself an epic of water
    flowing over
the indentations of each stone to lodge and change forever the
    course
the stone was set upon. I can tell you no more than this and so
    will repeat it
endlessly to myself and to whoever will listen – and do you listen
    or is this
not to your liking? Yes, the words were marching over the
    laws
of decorum and propriety and had nothing but themselves
    to answer to
and satisfy – that is if they chose to answer at all. And they
    didn't.
Their one concern was their own cadence and strange meanings

THE LANGUAGE OF WAVES

   I
was growing closer to but could not interpret in any tongue
   that is
common to us all unless it be that tongue which says what
   the waves
said to the stones and in which the stones replied

5
as the lighthouse beam pierced the dark again and the world
   drew substance
from that. That sudden illumination was everything the night
   aspired to
and to which, by these words, I also aspired. I was night walking
   the shore
which in daylight I'd walked so many times but never before in
   this particular
light. And it was beautiful. Yes, beautiful even among the passions
   of silence
which swept up the beach to counter the words but failed to dent
   the cadence
the words swung to. And yes, I was also swinging out on the
   lighthouse
light and waiting for it to return and tell me all that it saw and
   and then left
in the sudden dark I was back in but not in an unfriendly way
   and drew
substance from that – offered here in these words and in this cadence
   which I say
mirrors the sea and attempts to know the language of the waves.

TO THE HOUSE ON WHEELER HILL

TO THE HOUSE ON WHEELER HILL

To have built it – hands to a home, neighbours helping, the wood sawed to perfection – surely this must be the nineteenth century or what's left of it in the world?

The pastoral still captivates the heart. Poetry demands that lucidity and language is always open to the verbs of building and summer.

Dreams in wood become the house that was planned and built according to what the imagination is able to make solid in the world

And it is solid – the photographs show that – and I, yes, am somewhat envious of the life this pre-supposes and gives a form to

Yet the poem exonerates all guilt and longing. The house atones for all the years in which one has been unfaithful to its core – and what is its core?

It is fire and wood and the life that still says that the poem is possible in our time. Yes, this much and more and the wood speaks a language that can never be fully written but which must be lived down to the final degree

One thinks of beginnings. The pilgrim's dream. America before the fall. Yet this is also a beginning. Stories in wood that say the land is ripe for attention and the house is a statement of intent in an uncertain time

War in the world – voices rise from Iraq and Darfur and still the voice sings the lyric as if that was enough to offer a balm to the wounded.

It should always be so. The house should strengthen the heart and the voice articulate what the heart has set itself to.

This is poetry and justice. This is the lyric in its full flowering.

Therefore to you and yours these words are written and sent to Wheeler Hill. For justice, for love, for the endurance of the heart in a winter that needs Dante to describe it

May you all be well there. May the house endure and foster that life the house articulates. May justice show what can be done and may the heart do it.

May all the words of winter bow down to the verbs of spring.

YES

YES

To see it as a verb,
to write it in the affirmative,
to live in the now of yes,
to live in the now of us,
to make of the pronoun a verb,
to make of us a yes,
to trawl for light,
to know the star needs the darkness
to shine from,
to see the darkness & say yes,
to find it in the geography of no,
to see the yes embrace the no,
to see love as the perfect yes,
to wed my yes to yours, yes,
to wed, yes,
to live in the now of that,
to seek the solace of yes
in darker days,
to seek its accuracy,
to make a litany of yes
& recite it every day,
to adhere to it,
to suggested how it may be charmed
to a poem
which is to say to a life,
to savour its tangibility,
to savour its total otherness,
to bless you & drench you in it,
to make of it a measure,
to weigh all things by its gravity,
to make of it a mirror reflecting yes,
to make of it the pool of healing,
to bath in such waters
& emerge refreshed,

to savour it from the lips of the prophets,
to see all things with its piercing eye,
to see all things,
to say whatever you want to say by it
& no other,
to delve in its depths,
to find the deeper yes
echoing the surface one,
to speak it in all the languages,
to see & to name,
to name & to know,
to live in its present & future tense,
to adhere to its commands,
to live in the fullness of yes
as you pronounce it,
to accept no others before me,
to speak it loud & respond to its charge,
to say yes & yes & again yes,
to say yes & yes again.

ABOUT THE AUTHOR

Martin Burke was born in Ireland and now lives in Brugge, Belgium.

He was active in the poetry scene in Ireland in the early 70's with poetry published in the Stony Thursday Book (Limerick), New Irish Writing (Dublin) and New poetry (Cork).

On the move to Belgium poetry ceased and it is only in the past four years that it has once again returned. Since then he has published several books and has developed a style of writing that draws on the visionary poets of the total poetic tradition and this is one that allows him to bridge the gap between the written and the spoken – a development that culminated in the publication of KINGS-five poems for the theatre.

Indeed theatre is also a great love of his and he is in the process of setting up the Kosmos Theatre Group – a bilingual theatre group (English and Flemish) in Brugge.

www.ingramcontent.com/pod-product-compliance
Lightning Source LLC
Chambersburg PA
CBHW032133090426
42743CB00007B/585